THE UNOFFICIAL GUIDE TO
RESPONSIBLE BEHAVIOR IN MINECRAFT

JILL KEPPELER

PowerKiDS press

Published in 2026 by The Rosen Publishing Group, Inc.
2544 Clinton Street, Buffalo, NY 14224

Copyright © 2026 by The Rosen Publishing Group, Inc.

All rights reserved. No part of this book may be reproduced in any form without permission in writing from the publisher, except by a reviewer.

First Edition

Editor: Greg Roza
Book Design: Rachel Rising
Illustrator: Matías Lapegüe

Photo Credits: Cover, pp. 1, 3–24 SkillUp/Shutterstock.com; Cover, pp. 1, 3, 5, 7, 9, 11, 12, 15, 17, 19, 22, 23, 24 Oksana Kalashnykova/Shutterstock.com; Cover, p. 1 Soloma/Shutterstock.com; Cover, pp. 1, 3, 5, 7, 9, 11, 12, 15, 17, 19, 22, 23, 24 gersamina donnichi/Shutterstock.com; p. 21 Olena Yakobchuk/Shutterstock.com.

Cataloging-in-Publication Data

Names: Keppeler, Jill.
Title: The unofficial guide to responsible behavior in Minecraft / Jill Keppeler.
Description: Buffalo, New York : PowerKids Press, 2026. | Series: The unofficial guide to Minecraft social skills | Includes glossary and index.
Identifiers: ISBN 9781499452969 (pbk.) | ISBN 9781499452976 (library bound) | ISBN 9781499452983 (ebook)
Subjects: LCSH: Responsibility in children–Juvenile literature. | Responsibility–Juvenile literature. | Minecraft (Game)–Juvenile literature.
Classification: LCC BJ1451.K47 2026 | DDC 179'.9–dc23

Manufactured in the United States of America

Minecraft is a trademark of Mojang (a game development studio owned by Microsoft Technology Corporation), and its use in this book does not imply a recommendation or endorsement of this title by Mojang or Microsoft.

Some of the images in this book illustrate individuals who are models. The depictions do not imply actual situations or events.

CPSIA Compliance Information: Batch #CSPK26. For Further Information contact Rosen Publishing at 1-800-237-9932.

CONTENTS

IN A SHARED WORLD 4

ARE YOU RESPONSIBLE? 6

WHY BE RESPONSIBLE? 8

SHARING THE WORK 10

MAKING CHOICES 12

RESPONSIBILITY TO YOURSELF . . . 14

BEYOND CONTROL 16

OWN YOUR MISTAKES 18

WHEN A WORLD WORKS! 20

GLOSSARY. 22

FOR MORE INFORMATION 23

INDEX. 24

IN A SHARED WORLD

There's a sense of freedom in a new *Minecraft* world! There's nearly unlimited space to explore, countless **resources** to find, and nothing to stand in your way. (Except maybe monsters!) Everything is up to you. Want to tame an entire pack of wolves? You can do it! Want to **demolish** a mountain with TNT because it blocks your view? Go ahead!

But wait. You might want to play with friends, exploring the same world and working together—or competing. This changes a lot of things. Your behavior will affect more than you alone. You have a responsibility to those you're playing with.

MINECRAFT MANIA

 A *Minecraft* Realm is a **server** on which you can play with your friends. One of those friends (or likely a parent or other adult) will be the owner. They will need to invite people to play.

You can tame wolves in *Minecraft* by feeding them bones. Tamed wolves will attack monsters that attack you.

ARE YOU RESPONSIBLE?

Being responsible can mean a few different things. It can mean that people can trust you to do the things you're supposed to do. For example, imagine you're in a shared *Minecraft* world, and you said you'd find food while others started building a base. Being responsible means you'd do just that, instead of wandering off to explore.

Being responsible also means admitting your mistakes and fixing them. Imagine you put TNT in the wrong place and blew up part of a friend's base! You'd tell them you did it (instead of, say, blaming a monster) and get all the resources to repair the **damage** yourself.

MINECRAFT MANIA

 You can make a block of *Minecraft* TNT with four pieces of sand and five pieces of gunpowder. It can be useful for clearing land—but be sure you're not in the blast area!

TNT won't explode unless you light it (or some other form of fire or power touches it). Be careful if you have both a flint and steel and TNT in the supplies you're carrying!

WHY BE RESPONSIBLE?

It probably doesn't sound like much fun to be responsible. Maybe you changed your mind about gathering food and want to explore. And why be responsible for your mistake if you can just blame a creeper? But stop and think about it a minute. How would you feel about playing with someone who was acting that way? You probably wouldn't want to! You might wonder why you should be responsible if other people aren't.

But if everyone in your group decides to think this way, things can fall apart. This is just like how a real-world community works. Everyone needs to work together and be responsible for their part.

MINECRAFT MANIA

Each player in *Minecraft* has 20 hunger points. In most *Minecraft* **modes**, some actions will cause you to lose these points. You'll need to eat a food item to get them back. If they get too low, you'll lose health points!

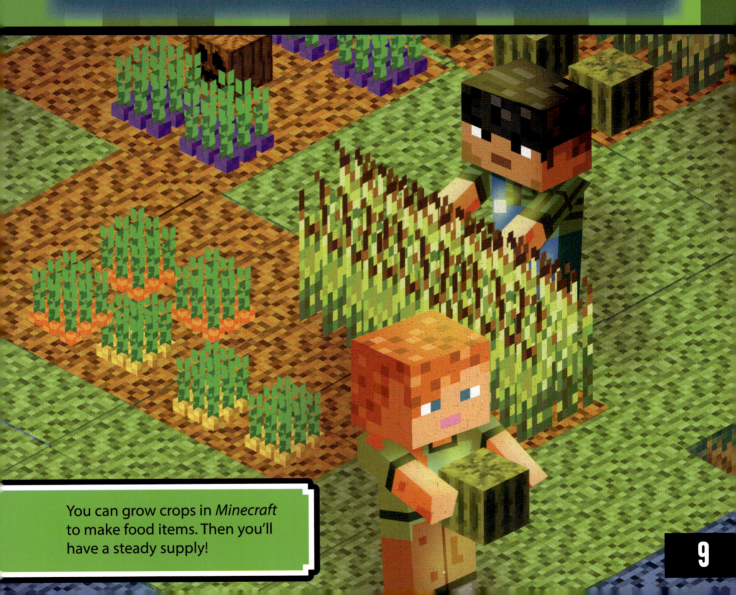

You can grow crops in *Minecraft* to make food items. Then you'll have a steady supply!

SHARING THE WORK

Being responsible doesn't mean doing everything yourself, though! Everyone needs to be responsible to make a world work. Responsibility may mean stepping up and being a leader. This could mean **assigning** jobs to people and making sure they do them. However, it could just mean doing your own job and doing it well.

Cooperation is important. This means working together to reach the same goal. The player who goes out and finds food for the players building a base is just as important as the ones doing the building. Other jobs, like gathering resources or protecting others from monsters, are also important.

MINECRAFT MANIA

 Most *Minecraft* monsters in the Overworld only **spawn** in darkness. Many also die in sunlight. Creepers, however, aren't bothered by daytime at all!

Protecting others is a big responsibility. They're trusting you to keep watch and keep them safe.

MAKING CHOICES

Being responsible can be a series of small choices. It may sometimes seem like only big choices are important, but this isn't true. Small choices add up! This is true both in *Minecraft* and in real life.

For example, imagine you go into your shared *Minecraft* world when your fellow players aren't there. Though you may be tempted, you choose not to look through their personal supplies. That's a responsible choice. You also choose to keep up your end of the Realm responsibilities by doing some building and exploring. That's another responsible choice. Of course, these will depend on the Realm rules the group has figured out.

MINECRAFT MANIA

It can be important to agree on rules for everyone playing in a Realm. Some basic rules might be no **griefing** and no stealing.

Griefing could include setting fire to a forest that other players are depending on for resources. Just like in the real world, fire can spread from tree to tree until there are none left.

RESPONSIBILITY TO YOURSELF

It might seem like responsibility is all about how you deal with others. This is part of it, but it's not the full story. Sometimes you have a responsibility to yourself to do the right thing. Being responsible also means taking care of your own stuff and owning your own actions. This includes keeping track of the resources you've gathered in *Minecraft* or putting away your own belongings in the real world.

Sometimes you could get away with being irresponsible … but do you want to? Just because you can do something doesn't mean you should. Imagine how your friends would feel if they found out. Proceed accordingly.

MINECRAFT MANIA

 To make a pair of linked ender chests in *Minecraft*, you need two eyes of ender and 16 blocks of obsidian. You can carry one chest with you and leave one in your base. That way, you can always get your stuff!

Like in the real world, in *Minecraft*, it can be upsetting to leave home and forget something you need. You can make linked ender chests to keep that from happening.

BEYOND CONTROL

Sometimes responsibility means recognizing that you can't control everything. You can avoid some problems by making the right choices, but sometimes it doesn't matter what you choose. You can only choose how you react to these problems.

This includes the actions of other people. Even if you have Realm rules, some people will choose not to follow them. They may try to get you to do this too. This, though, is in your power. You can't choose what other people do, but you can choose not to follow them. If some friends decide to damage another friend's base, you can choose not to take part. Resist pressure to do so.

MINECRAFT MANIA

 When *Minecraft* players are in a shared world, that world may be "owned" by one of them. If so, that person may have more control over the rules. You can still decide if you want to play with those rules, however.

You can do more than simply choose not to take part in breaking a server's rules. You can try to talk others out of doing so too.

OWN YOUR MISTAKES

An important part of being responsible is admitting your mistakes and fixing them as best you can. No one likes doing this! But it's also true that no one is perfect, and we all make mistakes. What's important is how we react to them. Try not to make excuses. Just **apologize**, mean it, and try to fix things.

Imagine that you accidentally left the gate to your shared base open, and a creeper got inside—and did what creepers do! Being responsible means apologizing and saying that you won't leave the gate open again. Then you gather all the supplies you need and fix the damage your mistake caused!

MINECRAFT MANIA

 How much damage a creeper explosion causes depends on the materials around it. Some materials have more blast resistance than others. This is how much it stands up to explosions.

Creeper holes—the pits they leave behind when they explode—can be very recognizable! They're usually deepest in the middle, where the creeper was standing.

WHEN A WORLD WORKS!

Being a responsible friend and *Minecraft* player may mean that people want to play with you more. You've shown that you can be trusted and that you respect others. In fact, others may act more responsibly because they see you doing so. This helps a *Minecraft* world work better for everyone.

Responsibility helps in the real world too. Responsible students do better in school and get along better with other people. They know how to meet their goals and take action. You might not think you're responsible, but responsibility is a skill that anyone can learn. Games like *Minecraft* can help you learn it!

Being responsible at home can show your parents or other adults that you're trustworthy and can have more freedom.

21

GLOSSARY

apologize: To say that you're sorry for something you've done.

assign: To give someone a task or amount of work to do.

damage: Loss or harm done to a person or piece of property; to do harm to a person or thing.

demolish: To tear something down or break it to pieces.

grief: To harass or annoy other players in *Minecraft* or other online games, just for fun and not as part of any attempt to play the game.

mode: A version, or form of something that is different from others.

resource: Something that can be used.

server: A computer in a network that provides services or files to others.

spawn: To first appear.

FOR MORE INFORMATION

BOOKS

Levy, Adir, and Ganit Levy. *What Should Darla Do? Featuring the Power to Choose.* Miami, FL: Elon Books, 2019.

Mojang AB. *Minecraft: Bite-Size Builds.* New York, NY: Del Rey, 2021.

Morlock, Rachael. *Hard Work and Determination: Developing Self-Discipline.* Buffalo, NY: PowerKids Press, 2019.

WEBSITES

Can Adults Do Whatever They Want?
wonderopolis.org/wonder/can-adults-do-whatever-they-want
Adults have to be responsible too! Learn more on Wonderopolis.

Realms
minecraft.wiki/w/Realms
Learn more about Minecraft Realms on the game wiki.

Publisher's note to educators and parents: Our editors have carefully reviewed these websites to ensure that they are suitable for students. Many websites change frequently, however, and we cannot guarantee that a site's future contents will continue to meet our high standards of quality and educational value. Be advised that students should be closely supervised whenever they access the internet.

INDEX

B

base, 6, 10, 15, 16, 18

C

choices, 12, 16, 17
cooperation, 10
creeper, 8, 11, 18, 19

E

explore, 4, 6, 8, 12

F

food, 6, 9, 10
friends, 4, 5, 6, 14, 16, 20

G

goals, 10, 20

M

mistakes, 6, 8, 18
monsters, 4, 5, 6, 10, 11

R

Realm, 5, 12, 16
resources, 4, 6, 10, 13, 14
rules, 12, 16, 17

S

shared/sharing, 4, 6,
10, 12, 18

T

TNT, 4, 6, 7